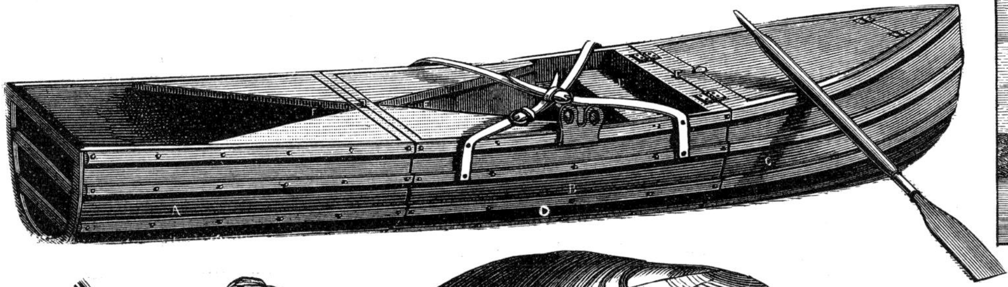

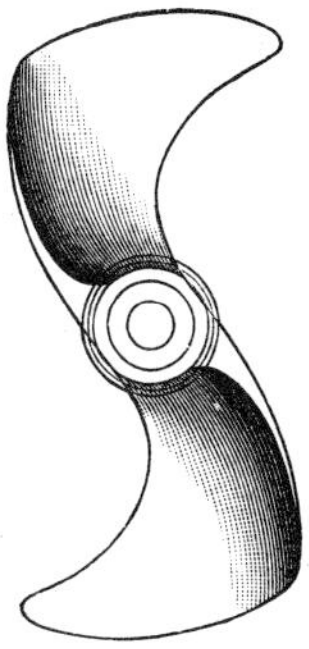

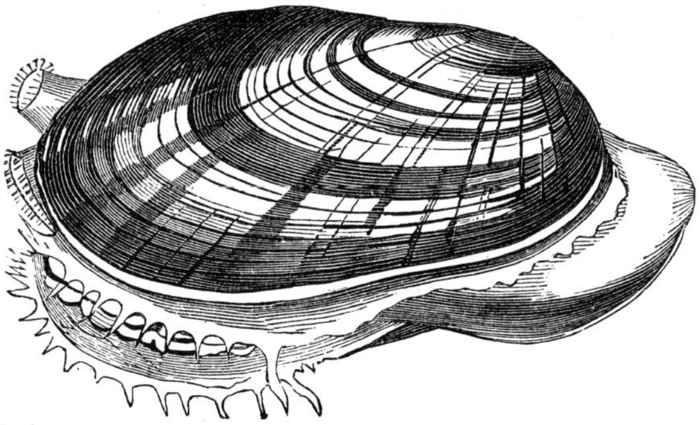

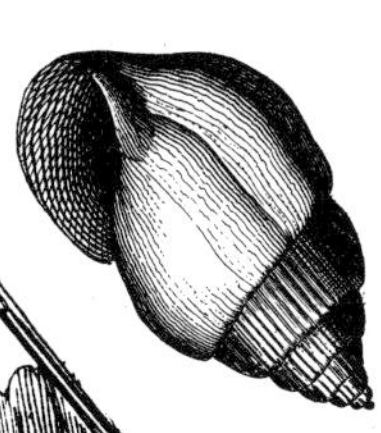

POYET

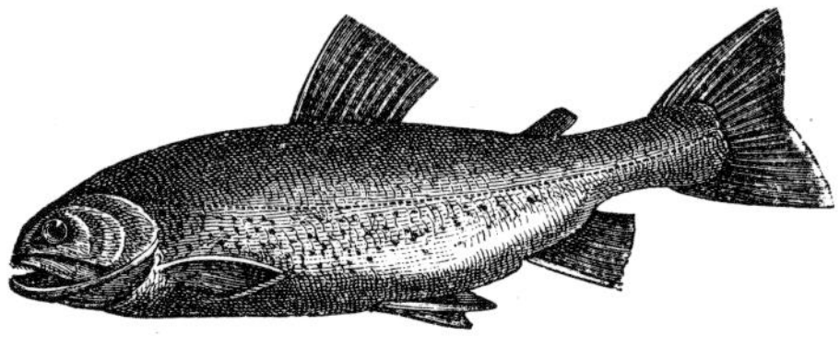

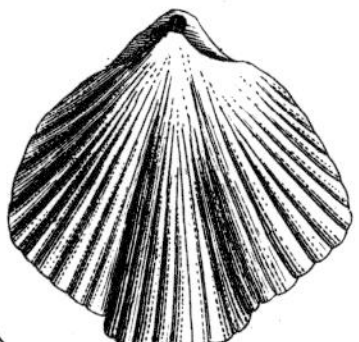

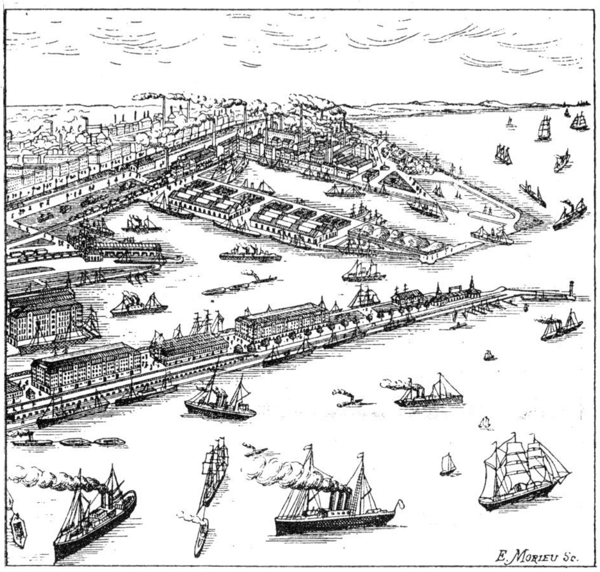
E. Morieu Sc.

To The
SUCCESS
ROYAL-LOUI
SIT LUX ET LUX FUIT
15
Step: Decatur
Commander
1781.

HERO

Shipped,

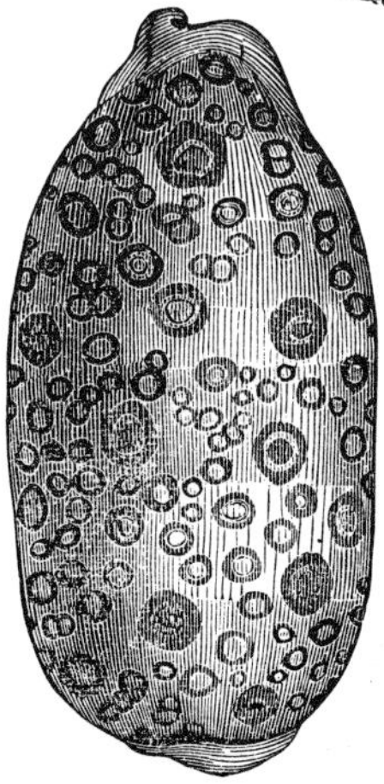

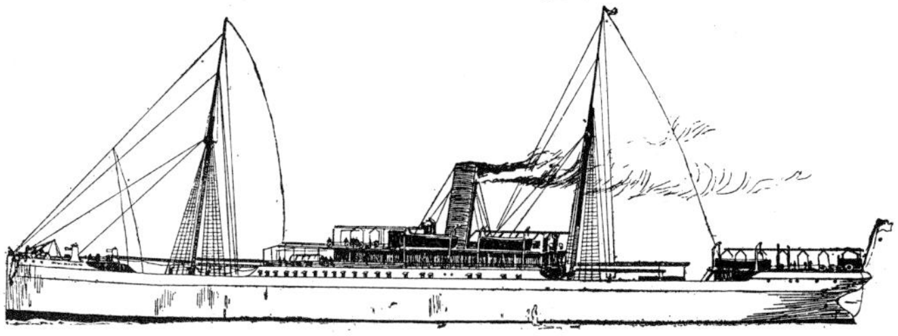

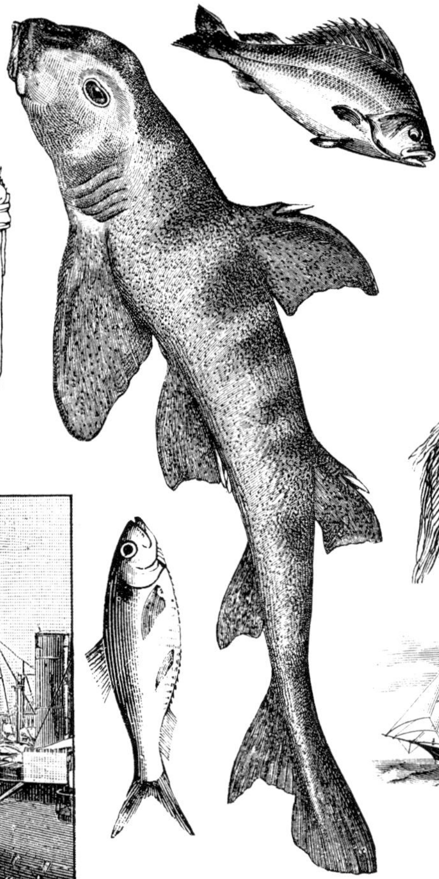

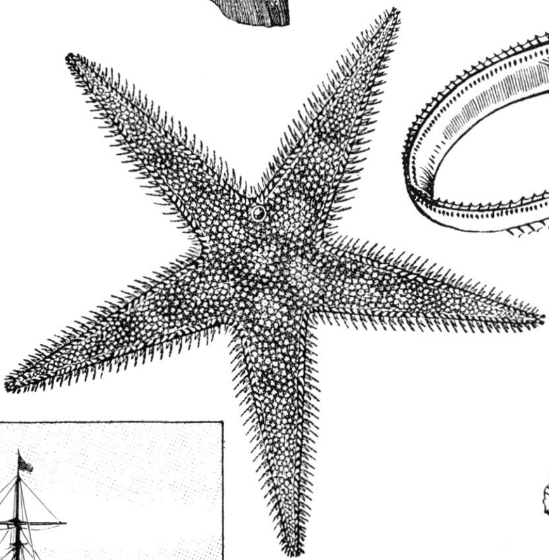
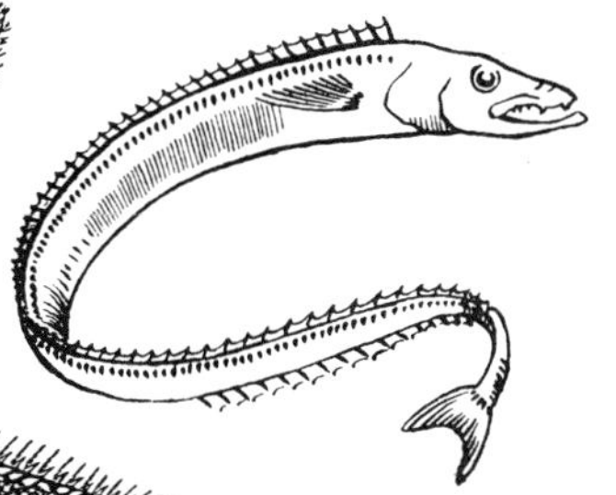

SHIPPED

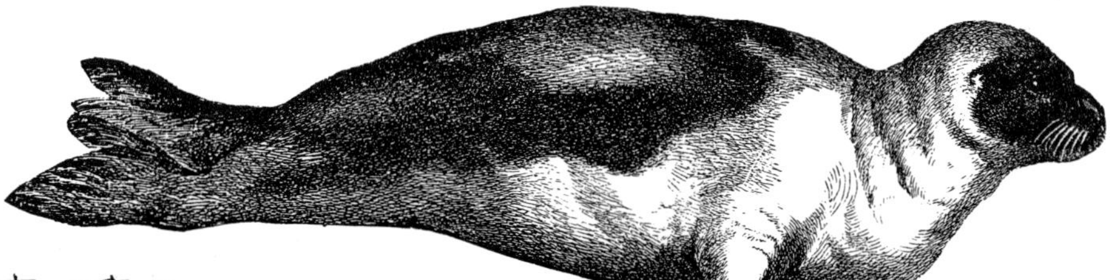

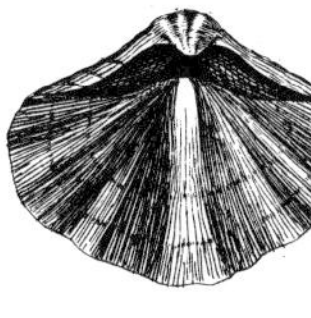

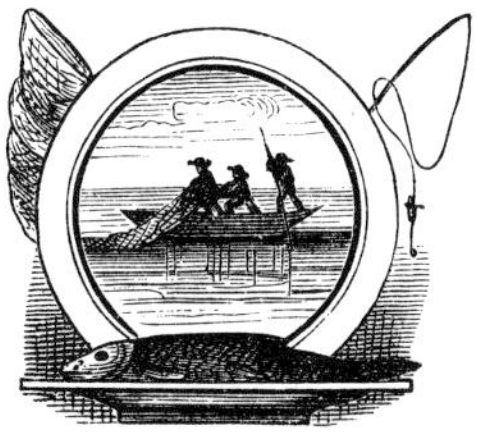

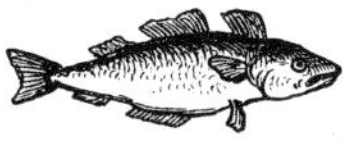
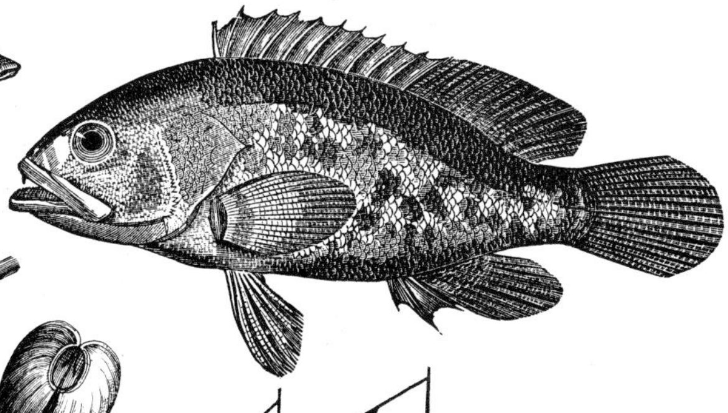

BELG
ANTWER

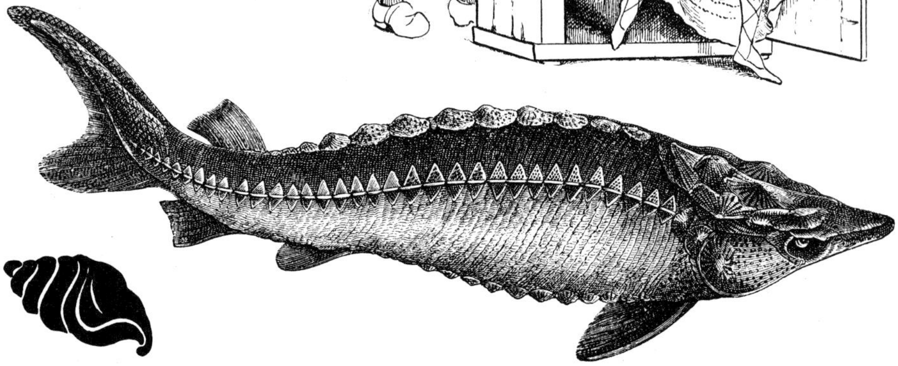

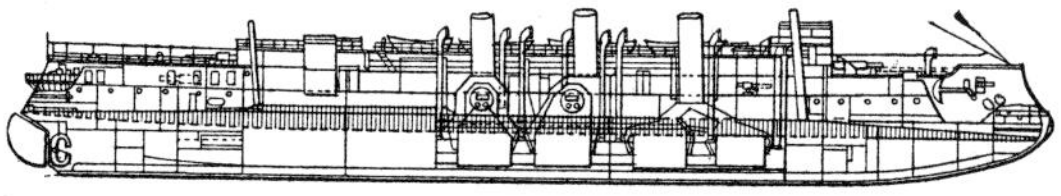

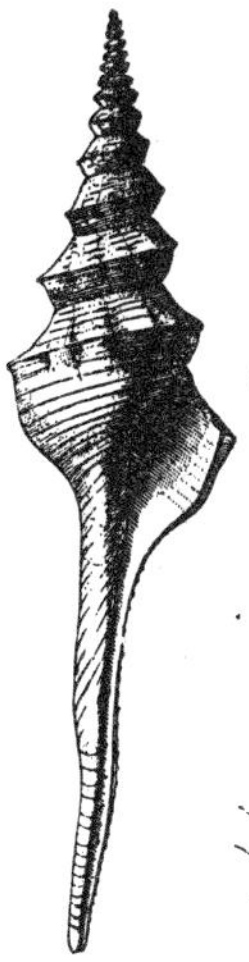

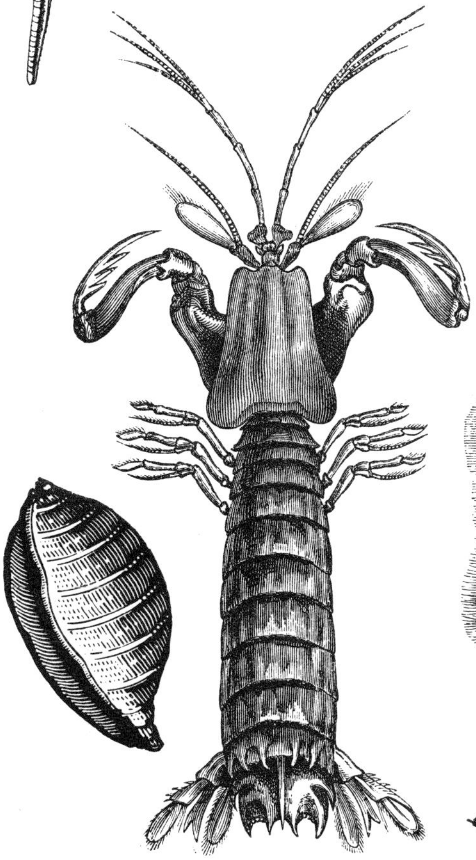

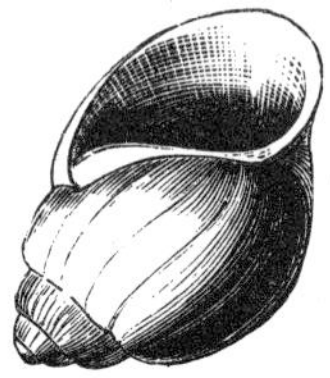

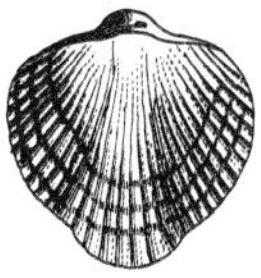

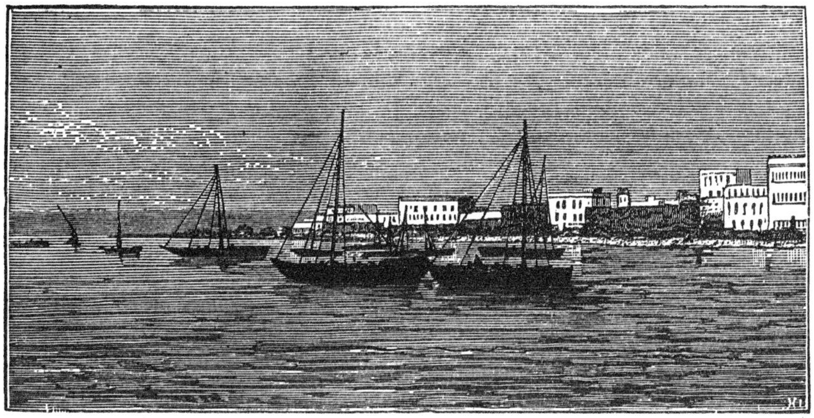

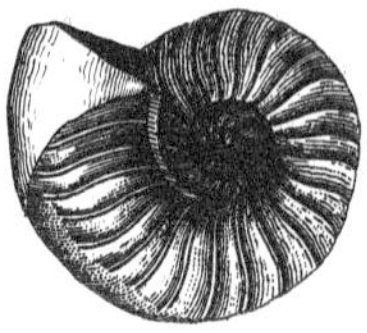

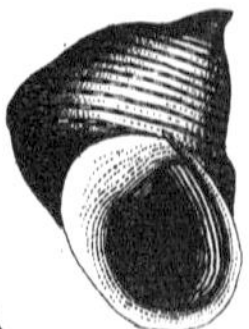

SHIPPED

ARCTIC NEW YORK

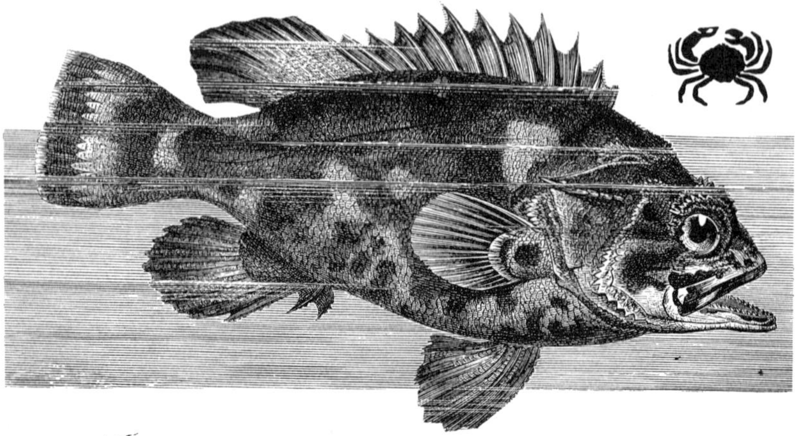
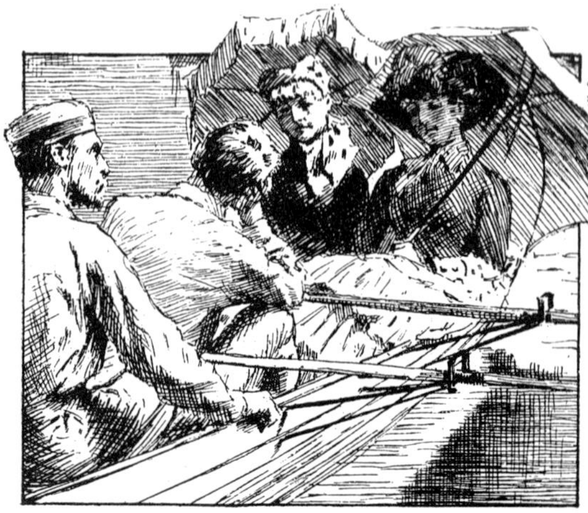

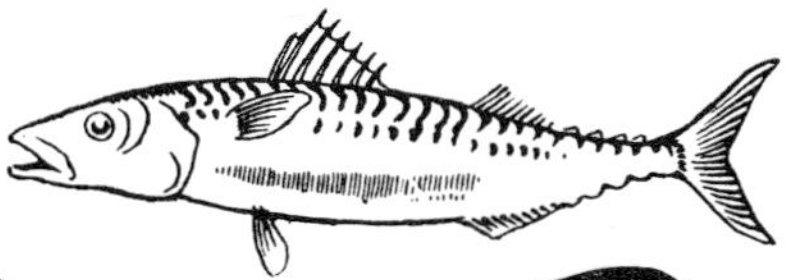

SHIPPED

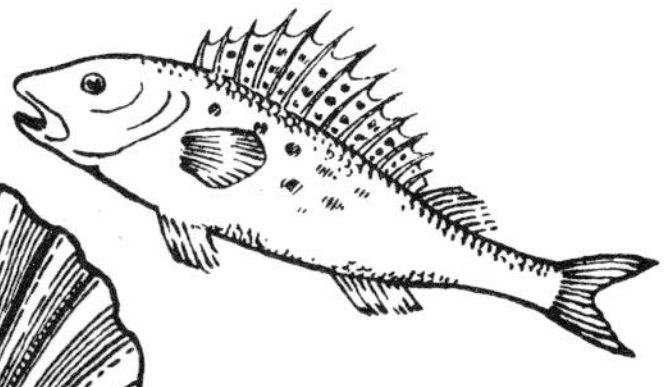

DAN BEARD

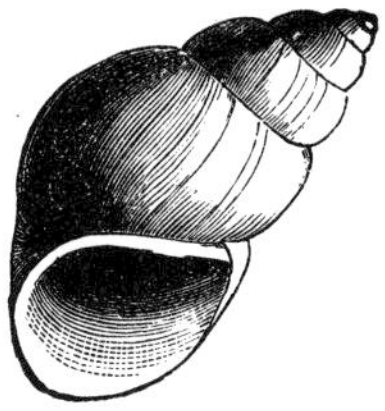

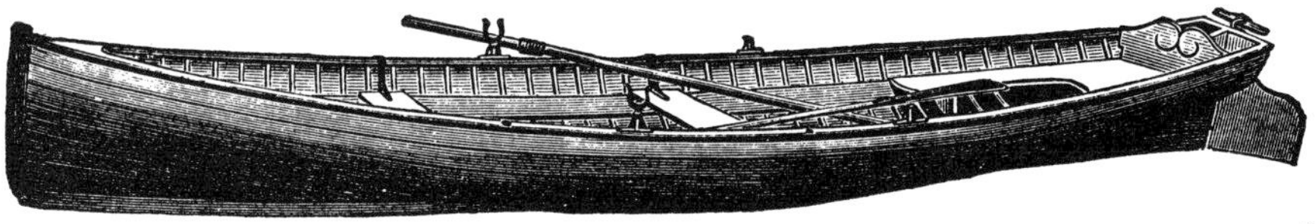

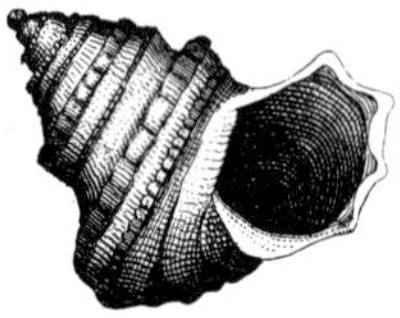

SHIPPED

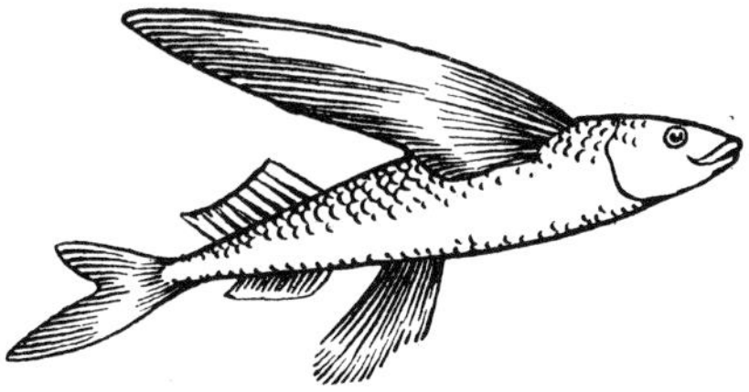

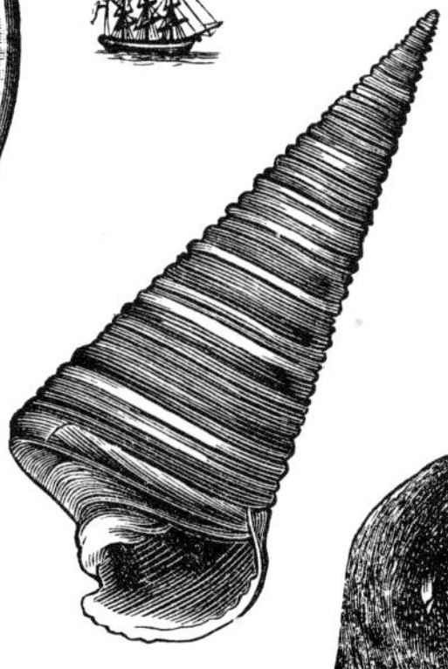

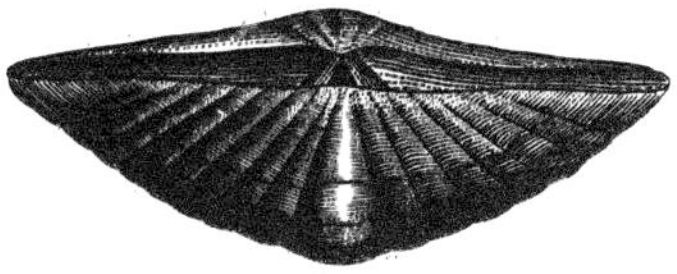

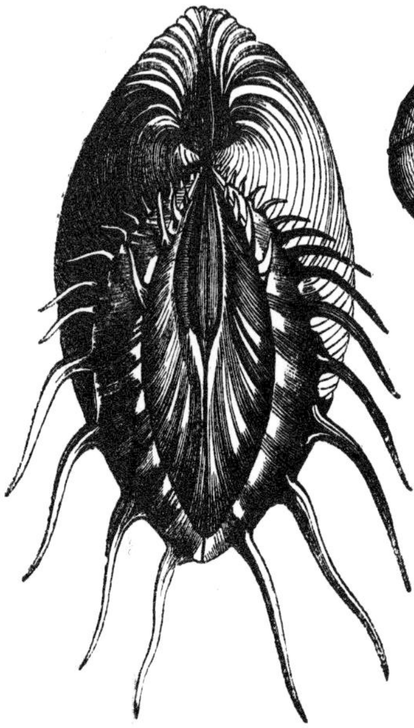
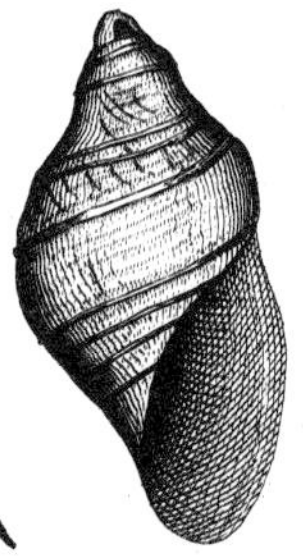
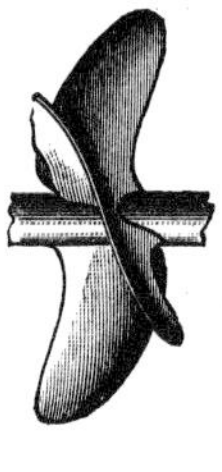

6

WHALER

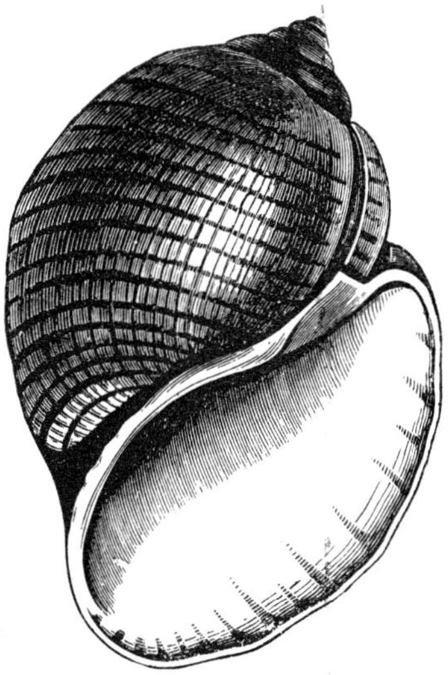

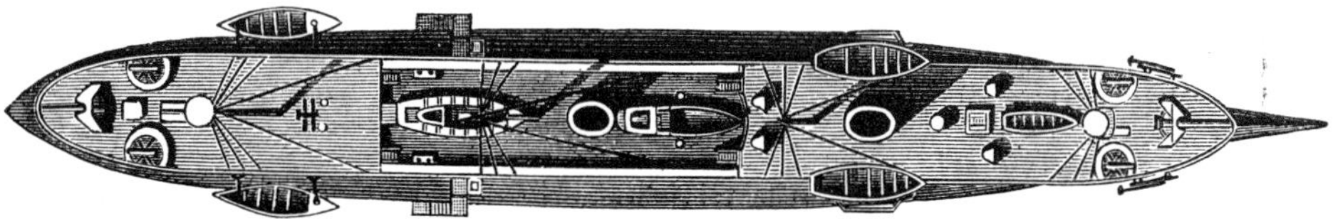

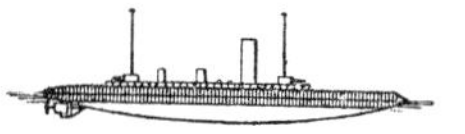

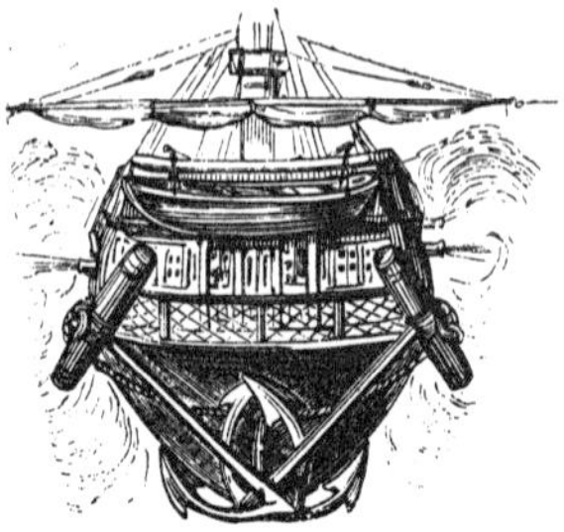

SVERRE SIGURDSON

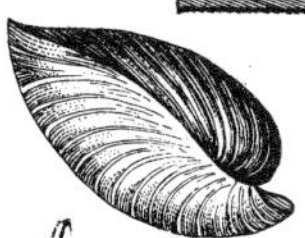
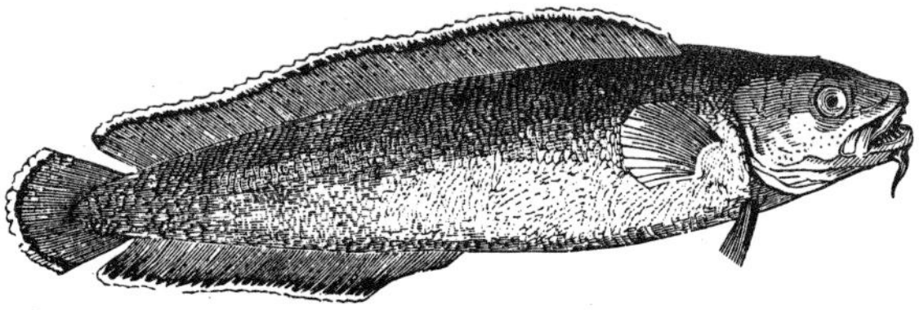

SPARTAN

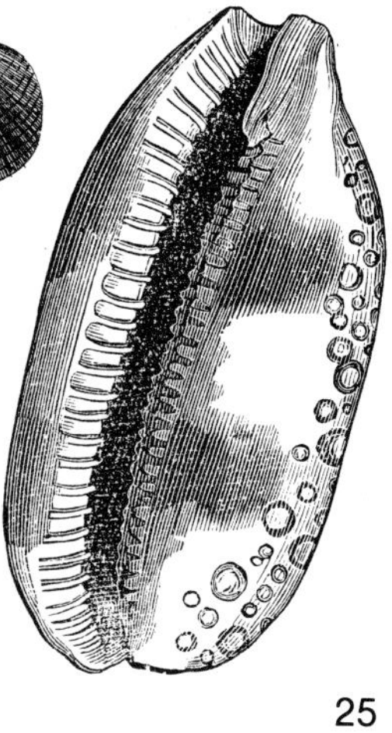

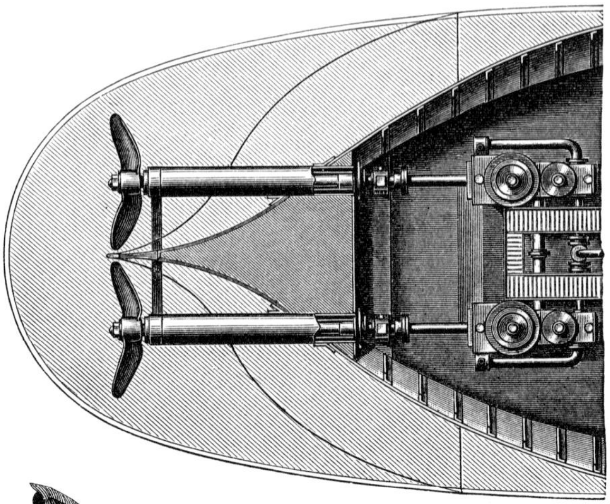
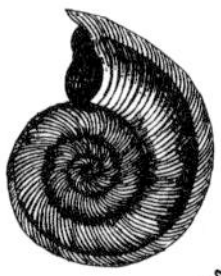

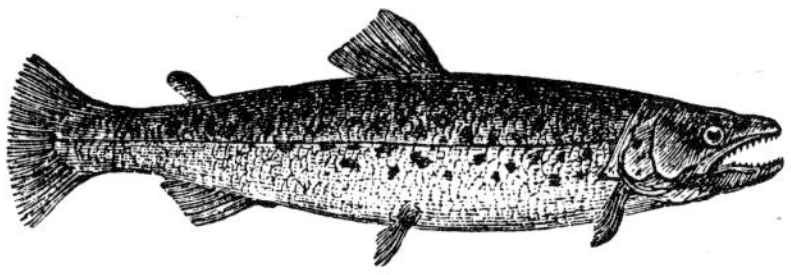

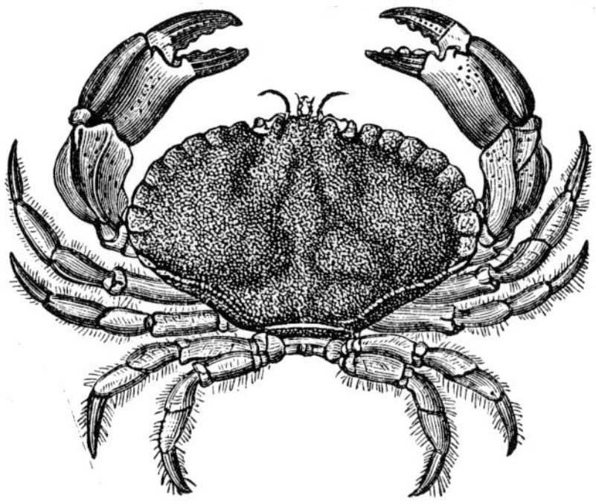

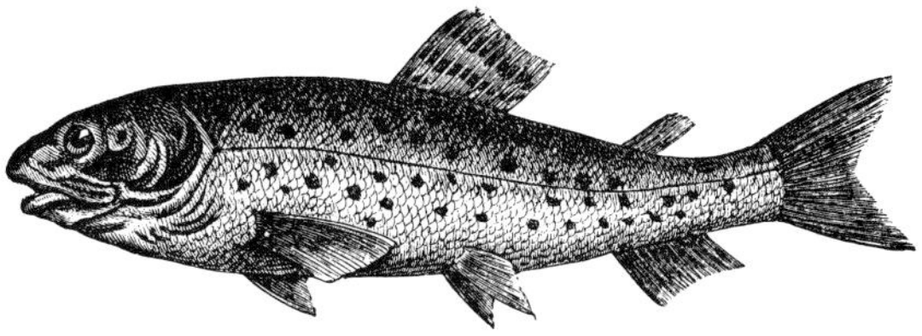

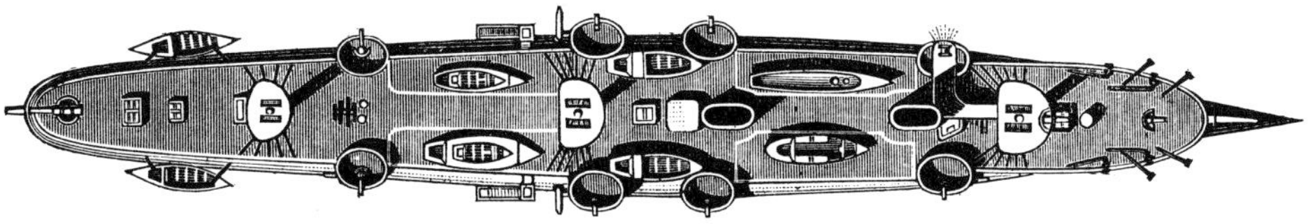

ELMIRA 2

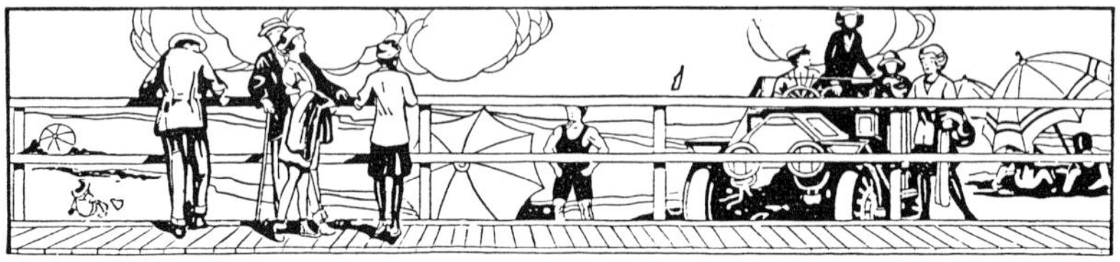

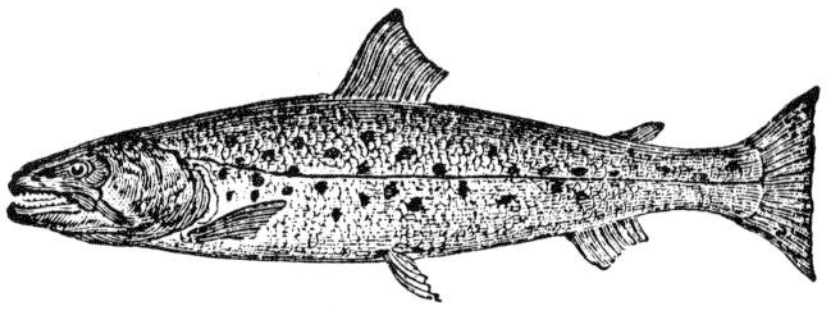

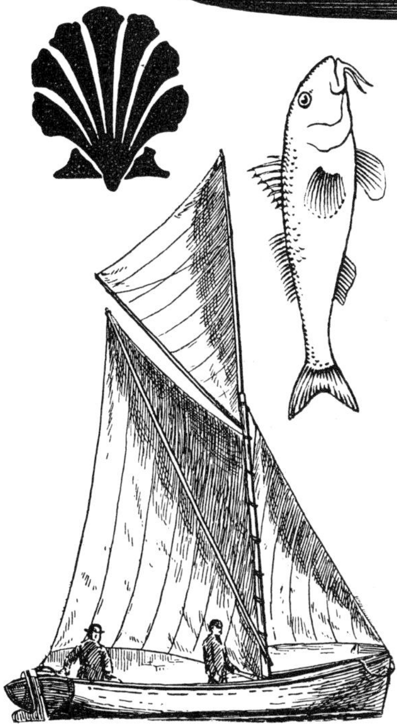

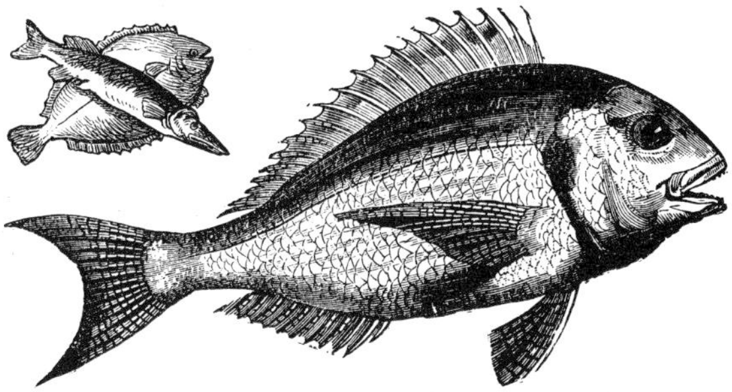

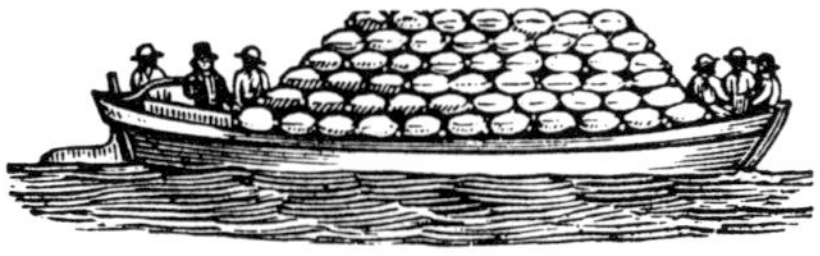

POYET

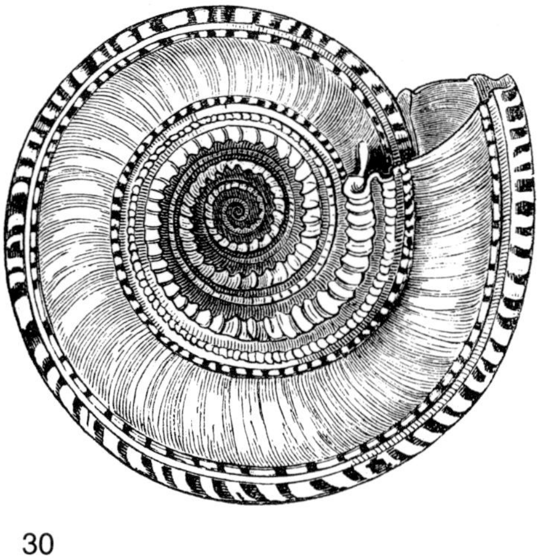

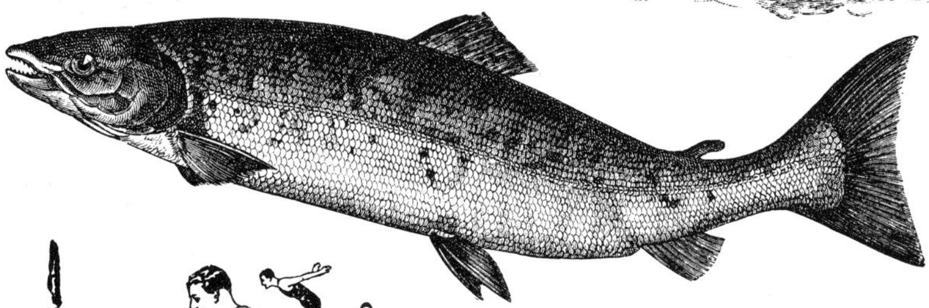

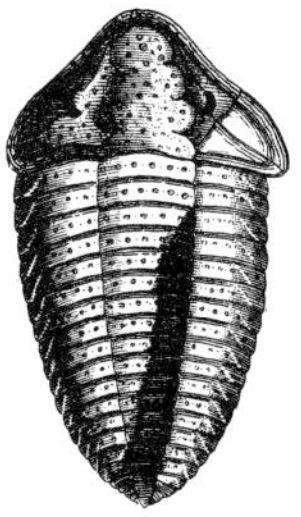
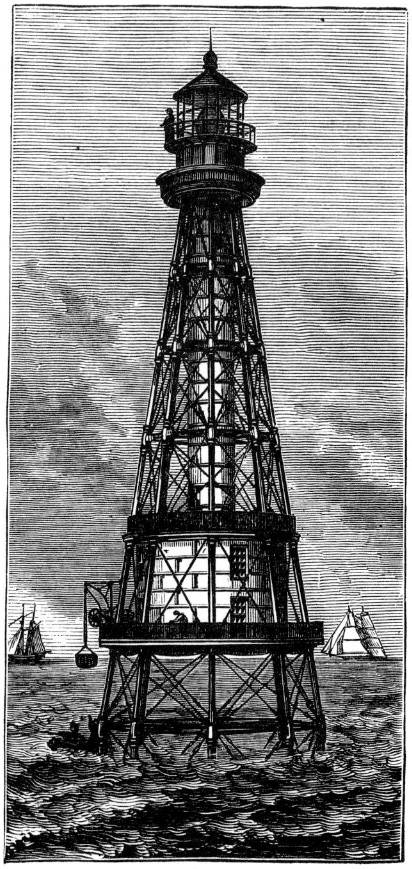

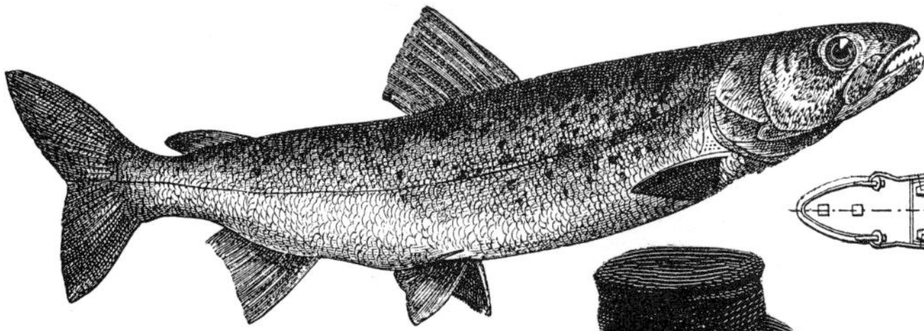
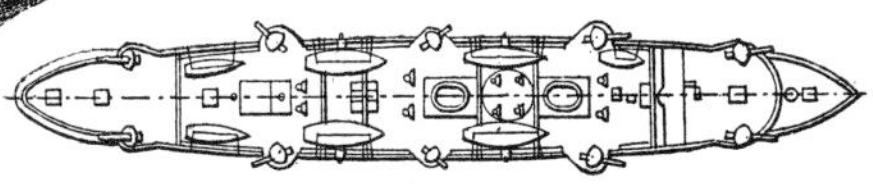

SHIPPED